Super Simple
Bend & Stretch

Healthy & Fun Activities to Move Your Body

Nancy Tuminelly

Contributing Physical Education Consultant, Linn Ahrendt, Power Play Education, Inc.
Consulting Editor, Diane Craig, M.A./Reading Specialist

A Division of ABDO

ABDO
Publishing Company

visit us at www.abdopublishing.com

Published by ABDO Publishing Company, a division of the ABDO Group, P.O. Box 398166, Minneapolis, Minnesota 55439. Copyright © 2012 by Abdo Consulting Group, Inc. International copyrights reserved in all countries. No part of this book may be reproduced in any form without written permission from the publisher. Super SandCastle™ is a trademark and logo of ABDO Publishing Company.

Printed in the United States of America, North Mankato, Minnesota
052011
092011

 PRINTED ON RECYCLED PAPER

Editor: Liz Salzmann
Content Development: Nancy Tuminelly, Linn Ahrendt
Cover and Interior Design and Production: Colleen Dolphin, Mighty Media, Inc.
Photo Credits: Colleen Dolphin, Shutterstock

The following manufacturers/names appearing in this book are trademarks: ACE®

Library of Congress Cataloging-in-Publication Data

Tuminelly, Nancy, 1952-
   Super simple bend & stretch : healthy & fun activities to move your body / Nancy Tuminelly.
      p. cm. -- (Super simple exercise)
   ISBN 978-1-61714-959-7
   1. Physical fitness for children--Juvenile literature. 2. Stretching exercises--Juvenile literature. I. Title.
   GV443.T85 2012
   613.7'042--dc22
                                                                    2011000963

Super SandCastle™ books are created by a team of professional educators, reading specialists, and content developers around five essential components—phonemic awareness, phonics, vocabulary, text comprehension, and fluency—to assist young readers as they develop reading skills and strategies and increase their general knowledge. All books are written, reviewed, and leveled for guided reading, early reading intervention, and Accelerated Reader® programs for use in shared, guided, and independent reading and writing activities to support a balanced approach to literacy instruction.

Note to Adults

This book is all about encouraging children to be active and play! Avoid having children compete against each other. At this age, the idea is for them to have fun and learn basic skills. Some of the activities in the book require adult assistance and/or permission. Make sure children play in appropriate spaces free of objects that can cause accidents or injuries. Stay with children at the park, playground, or mall, or when going for a walk. Make sure children wear appropriate shoes and clothing for comfort and ease of movement.

Contents

Time to Bend & Stretch!

Being active is one part of being healthy. You should move your body for at least one hour every day! You don't have to do it all at one time. It all adds up.

Being active gives you **energy** and helps your body grow strong. There are super simple ways to move your body. Two of them are bending and stretching. This book has fun and easy activities to get you started. Try them or make up your own.

Do You Know?
Being Active Helps You

1 be more relaxed and less stressed

2 feel better about yourself and what you can do

3 be more ready to learn and do well in school

4 rest better and sleep well at night

5 build strong bones, **muscles**, and joints

So turn off the TV, computer, or phone. Get up and start bending and stretching!

Muscle Mania

You have **muscles** all over your body. You use them whenever you move any part of your body. The more you move your muscles, the stronger they get!

shoulder

arm

neck

stomach

chest

back

upper leg

lower leg

Healthy Eating

You need **energy** to move your body. Good food gives your body energy. Some good foods are fruits, vegetables, milk, lean meat, fish, and bread. Foods such as pizza, hamburgers, French fries, and candy are okay sometimes. But you shouldn't eat them all the time.

Remember!

☑ Eating right every day is as important as being active every day

☑ Eat three healthy meals every day

☑ Eat five **servings** of fruits and vegetables every day

☑ Eat healthy snacks

☑ Eat fewer fast foods

☑ Drink a lot of water

☑ Eat less sugar, salt, and fat

Move It Chart

Make a chart to record how much time you spend doing things. Put your chart where you will see it often. This will help you remember to fill it out every day. See if you move your body at least an hour each day.

Move It Chart
Week of March 8-14

Activity	Sunday	Monday	Tuesday	Wednesday	Thursday	Friday	Saturday
volleyball							
Stretch It Out							
walk the dog							

1. Put the title of your chart at the top of a piece of paper. Then put "Week of" and a line for the dates.

2. Make a chart with eight **columns**. Put "activity" at the top of the first column. Put the days of the week at the top of the other columns. Under "activity," list all of the things you do. Include sports, games, and **chores**. Don't forget the activities in this book! Put "total time" at the bottom. Make copies of the chart.

3. Start a new chart each week. Put the dates at the top.

4. Mark how much time you spend on each activity each day. Be creative! Use different colors, **symbols**, or clock faces. For example, a blue sticker could mean 15 minutes of movement. A purple sticker could mean 60 minutes of movement.

    ◖ = 10 minutes   ◌ = 30 minutes

    ● = 15 minutes   ● = 60 minutes

5. Add up each day's activity. Did you move your body at least an hour every day?

Tools & Supplies

Here are some of the things you will need to get started.

music player

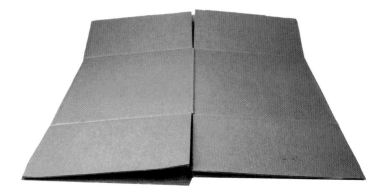

cardboard box with flaps

solid-colored yoga mat

markers

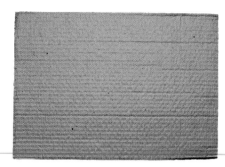

cardboard

old bath towels

stretch band

music

masking tape

puffy paint

chair

yardstick

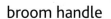

broom handle

Surf's Up!

Ride the waves on this surfboard!

WHAT YOU NEED
....

old bath towel
music player
surfer music
cardboard
markers

MUSCLES USED
....

leg
back
arm

TIME
....

5-10 minutes

1. Spread the **towel** on the floor. Start the music.

2. Hop up on your surfboard. Act like you are surfing. Bend your knees. Keep your feet apart. Use your arms to balance. Lean way to the left, and then to the right. Stand on one leg. Then **switch** legs. Try bending down low! Have fun moving all the parts of your body!

3. Paddle your board out to the waves! Lay on your stomach. Circle your arms in front of you. Kick your legs fast and then slow.

4. Try using a piece of cardboard for a surfboard. You could decorate it with markers.

Meow & Moo

Stretch and bend like a cat and a cow!

WHAT YOU NEED

solid-colored yoga mat
puffy paint

MUSCLES USED

shoulder
stomach
back

TIME

3-5 minutes

1. Use puffy paint to decorate your yoga mat. Make a fun border around the edge. Do not cover the whole mat with **designs**. Your hands and feet might slip on the paint.

2. Now try your meow and moo stretches. Lay the mat on the floor. Get on your hands and knees. Your knees should be under your hips. Your arms should be under your shoulders. Your neck should be straight so you are looking at the floor.

3. Breathe in. Pull your stomach in as far as you can. Count to five. Round your back like a cat. Your head will be looking down.

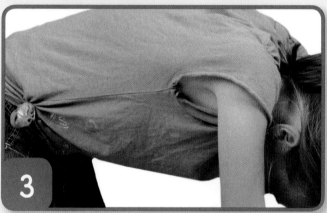

4. Breathe out. Let your stomach drop as far as you can. Count to five. Arch your back like a cow. Your head will be looking up.

Shoulder Rolls

This easy activity makes your shoulders strong!

WHAT YOU NEED

broom, mop,
   or 4-foot (1.2 m) stick

MUSCLES USED

arm

shoulder

stomach

back

TIME

3-5 minutes

1. Hold the broom over your head with your hands wide apart.

2. Drop your arms in front to your hips. Now bring your arms back up over your head.

3. Bend backward as far as you can. Bend your elbows. Bring the broom down behind your shoulders.

4. Then straighten and bring your arms back over your head.

5. Do Steps 2 through 4 five times.

6. Hold the broom with your hands closer together. Do Steps 2 through 4 five more times. Do you notice a difference?

➡ Keep moving your hands closer together. The closer your hands are together, the harder these stretches will be!

17

Stretch It Out

Work your muscles morning and night!

WHAT YOU NEED

chair

MUSCLES USED

leg
arm
shoulder
stomach
back
neck

TIME

5-10 minutes

1. Stand tall with your feet apart. Raise your arms over your head with your **palms** together.

2. Make small circles with your arms. At the same time, make circles with your hips. Try to circle your arms one way and your hips the other way!

3. Put one foot on the seat of a chair. Keep your knee straight. Bend over and see how far down your leg you can reach. Hold it for 10 seconds. Do the same with the other leg. Stretch on each side.

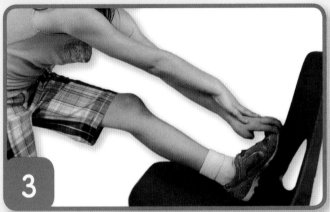

4. Sit on the floor with your legs straight in front of you. Bend and try to reach your toes. Hold for 10 seconds. Try to reach your hands around the bottom of your feet.

Stretch Test

Find out how flexible you are!

WHAT YOU NEED

cardboard box with flaps
masking tape
markers
yardstick or meterstick

MUSCLES USED

leg
stomach
back

TIME

3-5 minutes

1. Set the box upside down on the floor. Tape the **flaps** to the floor so the box won't move.

2. Sit down and put your feet against the box. Trace around your feet with a marker.

3. Tape the **yardstick** to the top of the box. It should stick out 20 inches (51 cm) from the edge of the box.

4. Sit on the floor. Put your feet against your **footprints**. The yardstick should be pointing toward you.

5. Bend at the **waist**. Reach forward. Try to keep your legs straight. Touch the yardstick. Measure how far you can reach. Can you reach all the way to the box? Try to put your hands flat on the top of the box.

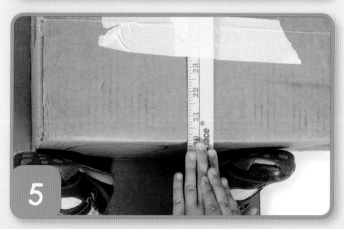

21

Teeter Totter

It's fun and easy to lift your friend in the air!

WHAT YOU NEED

just you and a friend

MUSCLES USED

leg
arm
stomach
back

TIME

5-10 minutes

1. Stand back-to-back with a friend. Hook your arms together at your elbows.

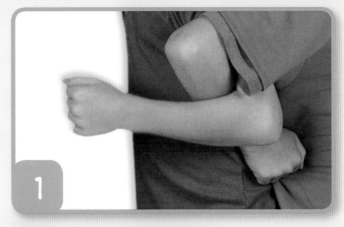

2. Bend your knees slightly. Slowly bend forward at the **waist**. Lift your friend off the floor.

3. Then slowly straighten up. Set your friend back on the floor.

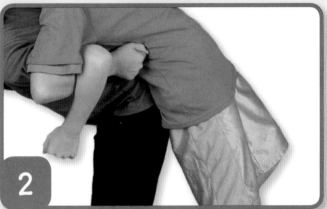

4. Then it's your friend's turn to lift you! Take turns lifting each other. Lift each other 10 times each.

....

➡ This activity works best if both people are about the same **height**.

....

23

Bendy Bands

Stretch all of your muscles at once!

WHAT YOU NEED

stretch band or elastic,
5 feet (1.5 m) long by
¾ inch (2 cm) wide

MUSCLES USED

arm
shoulder
stomach
back

TIME

5-10 minutes

1. **Arm curls:** Stand on the middle of the band. Hold one end in each hand. Slowly bring your hands up to your shoulders. Keep your elbows at your **waist**. Your **palms** should be facing up. Then slowly lower your arms down by your sides. Do this five times. Rest. Do five more arm curls.

2. **Side bends:** Fold the band in half. Hold one end in each hand above your head. Tighten your stomach **muscles**. Slowly bend to the left. Slowly straighten back up. Bend to the right the same way. Bend to each side five times.

3. **Shoulder presses:** Sit in the middle of the band. Hold one end in each hand. Raise your arms straight over your head. Your palms should be facing each other. Slowly bring your elbows down to your sides. Your hands should be at shoulder level. Slowly raise your hands back over your head. Do this five times. Rest. Do five more shoulder presses.

Balancing Act

Great stretches to work on your balance!

WHAT YOU NEED

just you

MUSCLES USED

leg
arm
shoulder
stomach
back

TIME

5-10 minutes

Leg Stand

1. Stand on one leg with your arms at your sides.

2. Bend the other leg back behind you. Hold your ankle or the top of your foot.

3. Pull your foot toward your bottom. Hold for 5 seconds. Try not to move or you may lose your balance! Put your foot back on the floor.

4. Do the same thing holding your other foot.

5. Do this stretch five times each way.

Rocking Horse

1. Stand on one leg with your arms at your sides.

2. Bend the other leg back behind you. Hold your ankle or the top of your foot.

3. Bend forward and touch the ground with your other hand. Try not to lose your balance!

4. Come back up slowly to where you started. Do the same thing holding your other foot. Do this stretch five times each way.

Body Board

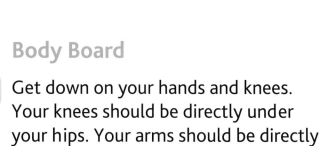

1. Get down on your hands and knees. Your knees should be directly under your hips. Your arms should be directly under your shoulders.

2. Raise one leg straight out behind you. Point your toes.

3. Lift the opposite arm straight out in front of you. Hold for 5 seconds. Lower your leg and arm. Do the same thing with the other leg and arm. Do this stretch five times each way.

Just Keep Moving!

Try these during TV and homework breaks, after meals, or anytime.

Saddle Stretch

Sit on the floor. Spread your legs wide apart. Lean forward with your arms straight. Put your hands on the floor. Hold for 3 to 5 seconds. Turn to the left. Grab your ankle or foot. Hold for 3 to 5 seconds. Turn to the right and repeat.

Twists

Stand with your feet apart. Raise your arms straight over your head. Twist the top of your body to the left. Go as far as possible. Do not move your hips or knees. Then twist to the right. Do this five to 10 times on each side.

Wall Squats

Stand with your back against a wall. Place your feet about 12 inches (30 cm) out from wall. Bend your knees so your back slides down the wall. Go down as far as you can. Hold for 10 to 15 seconds. Then come back up slowly. Do this for 1 to 3 minutes.

Being active is for everyone!

- Ask your family to join in activities at home.
- Have relay races with your classmates at recess.
- Have an adult take you to a safe park to play tag with friends.

Super Simple Moves
Pledge

I promise to be active and move my body for one hour a day, five days a week.
I know that eating right and getting enough sleep are also important.
I want to be healthy and have a strong body.

I will:

☑ keep track of my activities on a Move It Chart or something like it

☑ ask my friends to stay active with me and set up play times outside three days a week

☑ ask my family to plan a physical activity one day a week

☑ limit my time watching TV and using the computer, except for homework

☑ get up and move my body during TV commercials and homework breaks

To print a pledge certificate, go to www.abdopublishing.com.
For more information about being active, please visit www.letsmove.gov.

Glossary

chore – a regular job or task, such as cleaning your room.

column – one of the vertical rows in a table or chart.

design – a decorative pattern.

energy – the ability to move, work, or play hard without getting tired.

flap – a flat, movable part that hangs from the side of something.

footprint – a mark or track made by a foot or shoe.

height – how tall something is.

muscle – the tissue connected to the bones that allows body parts to move.

palm – the inside of your hand between your wrist and fingers.

serving – a single portion of food.

switch – to change from one thing to another.

symbol – an object or picture that stands for or represents something.

towel – a cloth or paper used for cleaning or drying.

waist – the area of your body between your chest and hips.

yardstick – a measuring tool that is one yard long and marked in feet and inches.